THᴱ

Fa
M
Ma
dec
hav
size...   ...ng collection extending
from the seventeenth century to the middle
of the twentieth century.

The most outstanding group of fans are
those with royal connexions. A large num-
ber of royal items have been incorporated
into the Museum's collections as loans or
gifts as the result of George V's involve-
ment in founding the London Museum at
Kensington Palace. Both Queen Alexandra
and Queen Mary took a lively interest in
the Museum, particularly the costume
collection, and helped to lay the founda-
tions of the Museum's royal collection.
This material has in turn attracted many
other items of royal personalia, including fans
decorated or owned by members of the royal
family, or presented to them. Popular fans
commemorating royal events are also
included in the collection.

It is appropriate that the fan collection
should reflect the Museum of London's
main concern with the history of the Capital.
Although some fans commemorating events
or activities in London were acquired in the
Museum's earliest days – two engraved
Bartholomew Fair fan leaves, for instance –
it is only recently that many more such
London or commemorative fans have been
collected. Preparations for the 1985/86
exhibition, with which this publication is
linked, highlighted many such gaps in the
collection and several fans have been
acquired to remedy the situation. The
Museum will be continuing to collect fans of
all kinds since they form an important adjunct
to the fine dresses in the costume collection,
and are also most attractive and relevant
memorials of London's past history.

Recent discoveries of worked bone and tortoiseshell sticks and guards in archaeological

Front cover
*Large fan with a leaf formed of silk 'petals'
painted with lilies of the valley and bunches of
roses, thistles and shamrocks; the sticks and
guards are of intricately pierced and carved mother
of pearl. Queen Victoria's crown and cipher and
the date 24 May 1858 on the central panels suggest
that this may have been a present to the Queen on
her 39th birthday.*

*Smaller fan of 1895–1905 with irises painted in
gouache on the silk leaf by I Gerard; the composition sticks and guards imitate amber and are
studded with steel spangles. The fan originally
belonged to Princess Helena Victoria, a grand-
daughter of Queen Victoria, and is also signed
'Duvelleroy'.*

*Small closed fan of 1828, pierced and carved gilt
metal guards enriched with semi-precious stones.*

Inside cover (left)
*Large 1920s fan of trimmed and curled green
ostrich feathers, with composition sticks and
guards imitating amber.*

*Fixed fan of swansdown ornamented with a hum-
ming bird, with turned bone handle. Part of the
ensemble worn to the Waverley Ball in 1871 by
Alexandra, Princess of Wales as 'Mary, Queen
of Scots'.*

*Small fan of guinea fowl and white duck feathers
with mother of pearl sticks and guards, 1870–90.*

*1 Fan design, by an unknown artist, in pen, ink
and grey wash on paper. This illustrates part of
the 1686 inaugural procession of the Lord Mayor,
Sir John Peake, when the Chariot of the Virgin
Queen (the symbol of Peake's Livery Company,
the Mercers') passed through the Stocks Market
in the City of London on 29 October. The Virgin
Queen is surrounded by her attributes – Fame,
Vigilance, Hope, Faith, Wisdom and Chastity –
and the chariot is led by Triumph, a Roman
charioteer. (above)*

Back cover
*Fan design of 1728–30 showing St Bartholomew's
Fair, etching and aquatint (coloured) published
by J F Setchel, 23 King Street, Covent Garden.
The original watercolour design for a fan to be
sold at the Fair is in the British Museum. Founded
in the twelfth century, the Fair was held annually
in Smithfield and was one of the great medieval
cloth fairs of England. After the Restoration it
was mainly given over to small booths and side
shows; it ended in 1855.*

2 Late seventeenth century French fan of vellum painted in gouache colours with a design showing fruit and flowers being offered to a god; the reverse is embellished with a floral design. The carved ivory sticks are slotted into the leaf, a feature more usual in earlier fans.

deposits in London offer intriguing possibilities for further research into this minor London industry as well as new evidence for attributions and dating.

THE MUSEUM OF LONDON
1985

The Museum of London is funded by the Office of Arts & Libraries, the Greater London Council and the Corporation of the City of London

© *Copyright Museum of London 1985*

Text by Kay Staniland
Edited by Valerie Cumming
Photography by Susan E Seright
Designed by David Challis
Printed in England by Jolly & Barber Limited, Rugby
ISBN 0 904818 18 7

FANS

The origin of the fan is still obscure. Devised in hot climates as an instrument for agitating the air, it eventually became a highly ornate status symbol as well, a mass of colourful feathers and sparkling gems set in precious metals. These attractive novelties appeared in Europe in the mid-sixteenth century and are often to be seen in portraits of Elizabeth I and the ladies of her Court. This fixed fan was gradually eclipsed by the folded fan, introduced, it is believed, from the Far East. The few surviving sixteenth century folding fans have elaborately pierced or decorated leaves threaded onto sticks.

Vellum and paper became the usual materials for the fan leaf, offering exciting possibilities for elaborate decoration in miniature. Continental artists took full advantage of the new art form, spreading their designs, taken principally from manuscripts and tapestries, over the whole leaf. Subjects were generally derived from well-known classical mythology or biblical stories and, much more rarely, from contemporary life. Fans continued as desirable but very expensive feminine accessories: the perquisite of the rich they were frequently attacked as unnecessary extravagances. A writer in 1641, for instance, bitterly criticised the vanity of the daughters of churchmen 'walking in Cheapside with their fannes and farthingales'.

It is not known when fans were first manufactured in England, but the influx of Huguenot refugees after 1685 clearly gave the craft a considerable boost. By 1709 there were sufficient craftsmen in London and the surrounding area to warrant the establishment of a Fan Makers' Company in London. The industry already consisted of such specialists as stickmakers and fan painters. Fan making flourished in London and a distinctive English style was gradually evolved.

3 Dutch fan of 1735–45 with pierced and carved
ivory sticks embellished with colours. The paper
leaf is painted in gouache with a conversation piece
set in a garden; the ladies hold fans, while
a serving maid brings glasses and wine
bottles. The reverse has a small
landscape design.

4 Heading for a trade bill issued in 1751 by
Bar, Fisher & Sister who 'Sold all Manner
of Fans Wholesale & Retail. Likewise
Lace, Childbed Linnen & all kinds of
Millinary. Lace join'd & mended,
Fans Mounted, mended &c.'

5 A special display of fireworks
was held in Green Park on 27 April 1749
to commemorate the Peace of Aix-la-Chapelle
which ended the War of Austrian Succession in 1748.
This fan is a souvenir of that occasion, an early example
of an engraved English fan leaf to which coloured washes have
been added. The bone sticks and guards have painted decoration in
pink and blue on a sponged sea green ground. George II commissioned the
famous 'Music for the Royal Fireworks' from Handel for this occasion.

4

🐾 Despite the imposition of heavy duties, imports continued to predominate, a situation reflected in the Museum's collection. English taste was much influenced by the Continent and fans, together with such other fashionable luxuries as lace and brocaded silks, were probably smuggled into England in some quantity. It was the expanding trading activities of the East India Company which most radically affected the market for fans in Europe. Together with the other Eastern commodities like tea, rice and porcelain which were rapidly becoming necessities rather than occasional luxuries, the Company imported increasing quantities of oriental paper fans. These were specially decorated to suit the European concept of oriental design. The flood of these cheap fans, together with home-produced copies, often equally cheap, soon made the fan a necessary accessory for any lady with fashionable or social pretensions. 'The ladies gave me a gale with their fans' Jonathan Swift makes Gulliver comment in 1727.

6 *English paper fan of 1770–80 painted with a chinoiserie design in gouache on a silver ground; the reverse has a flower spray. The carved and pierced ivory guards are ornamented with mother of pearl chips. The fan has its own embossed and printed card box with the label of 'Clarke, Fan Maker, No. 27, near Hungerford Street, Strand, London.' (above, left)*

7 *'Grand Tour' fan, a souvenir of the 1770s from Italy. The kid leaf is painted with medallions showing tourists visiting three Roman ruins, surrounded by classical motifs, in coloured gouache. The bone sticks are pierced and the guards show a fashionable lady seated by an urn. Formerly owned by Princess Alice, Countess of Athlone. (left)*

As the eighteenth century progressed the products of London fan makers could be of as high a quality as those of their foreign competitors, although it became increasingly necessary to suit style and subject to the English taste. The wide popularity of fans produced a demand which only greater division of skills and the adoption of mass-production techniques could fulfil. London's many skilled craftsmen were dismayed by the appearance of quantities of engraved fan leaves in the 1730s, but these cheap and topical fans satisfied only a part of the market.

Changes in fashionable styles were reflected in dresses and their accessories, and fans changed considerably towards the end of the eighteenth century. Rich embellishment gradually subsided, and ornament was confined within cartouches. Borders were simplified, colours became muted and new subjects were introduced.

8 French fan of 1775–85, the carved and pierced ivory sticks embellished with gold and silver leaf and spangles. The finely painted central motif shows a pair of lovers in a rural setting flanked by symbols of Mars and Venus, and putti in medallions. (above)

9 This fan of printed paper enriched with coloured washes and silver spangles commemorates two unmanned balloon flights. The ascent of 'Messr Charles and Roberts Balloon' in Paris on 27 August 1783 is in the centre. The side medallions probably commemorate the flight of Michael Biaggini's second balloon, released from the Artillery Ground at Moorfields on 25 November 1783. Biaggini, an artificial flower maker of Cheapside, made this balloon of oiled yellow silk, 10 ft. in diameter, in collaboration with Count Francesco Zambeccari. It descended 2¼ hours later, 48 miles away near Petworth in Sussex. (right)

10 Ivory fan made in China, for the Western market, in the mid-eighteenth century. The pierced sticks have medallions of Chinese scenes painted in colours on both sides and the guards are carved with Chinese scenes and motifs. (left)

11 'The Lady's Adviser, Physician and Moralist: or Half an Hours Entertainment at the Expence of Nobody', an unmounted paper fan leaf of 1797 printed in black. One of a group of witty topical leaves published for cheap fans by the firm of Sarah Ashton of No.28 Little Britain. (below)

12 Pierced ivory guard from an Italian fan of 1780–90. (right)

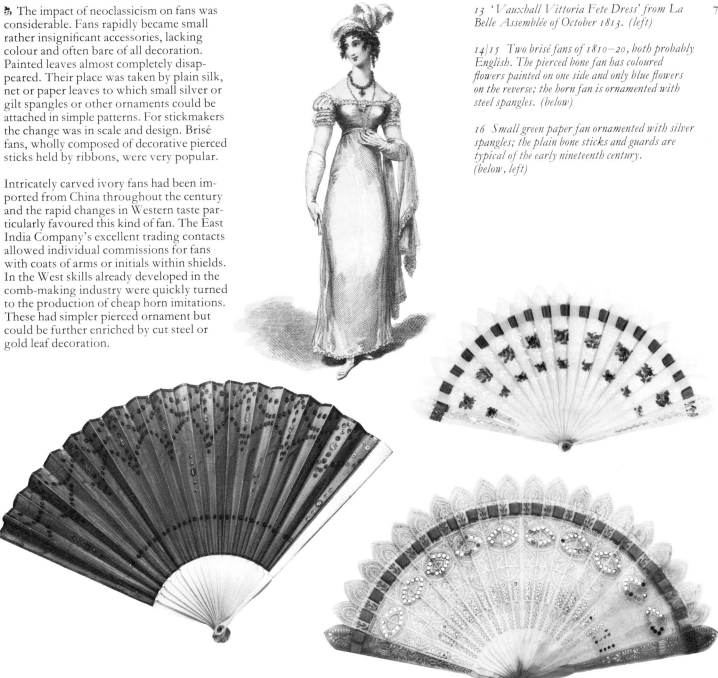

The impact of neoclassicism on fans was considerable. Fans rapidly became small rather insignificant accessories, lacking colour and often bare of all decoration. Painted leaves almost completely disappeared. Their place was taken by plain silk, net or paper leaves to which small silver or gilt spangles or other ornaments could be attached in simple patterns. For stickmakers the change was in scale and design. Brisé fans, wholly composed of decorative pierced sticks held by ribbons, were very popular.

Intricately carved ivory fans had been imported from China throughout the century and the rapid changes in Western taste particularly favoured this kind of fan. The East India Company's excellent trading contacts allowed individual commissions for fans with coats of arms or initials within shields. In the West skills already developed in the comb-making industry were quickly turned to the production of cheap horn imitations. These had simpler pierced ornament but could be further enriched by cut steel or gold leaf decoration.

13 'Vauxhall Vittoria Fete Dress' from La Belle Assemblée of October 1813. (left)

14/15 Two brisé fans of 1810–20, both probably English. The pierced bone fan has coloured flowers painted on one side and only blue flowers on the reverse; the horn fan is ornamented with steel spangles. (below)

16 Small green paper fan ornamented with silver spangles; the plain bone sticks and guards are typical of the early nineteenth century. (below, left)

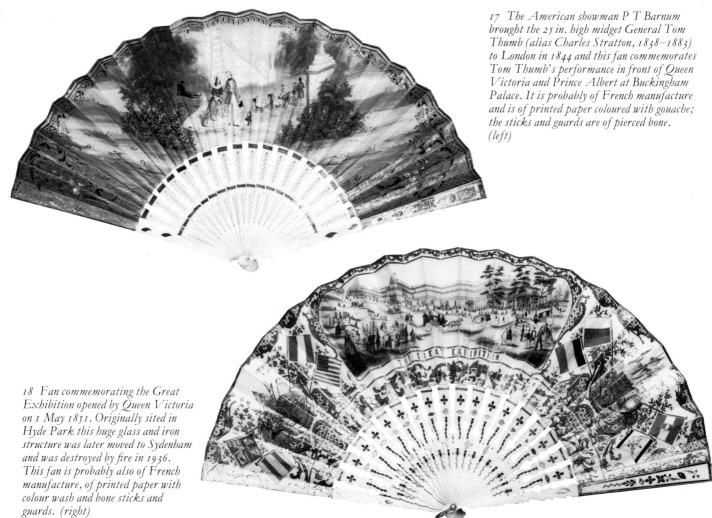

17 *The American showman P T Barnum brought the 25 in. high midget General Tom Thumb (alias Charles Stratton, 1838–1883) to London in 1844 and this fan commemorates Tom Thumb's performance in front of Queen Victoria and Prince Albert at Buckingham Palace. It is probably of French manufacture and is of printed paper coloured with gouache; the sticks and guards are of pierced bone. (left)*

18 *Fan commemorating the Great Exhibition opened by Queen Victoria on 1 May 1851. Originally sited in Hyde Park this huge glass and iron structure was later moved to Sydenham and was destroyed by fire in 1936. This fan is probably also of French manufacture, of printed paper with colour wash and bone sticks and guards. (right)*

As colour and pattern gradually returned to fashionable dress, they reappeared in fan design too. Fans began to grow in size during the 1820s and soon returned to the earlier proportions. Nostalgia for the past brought an even stronger reliance on earlier decorative traditions, translated to suit Victorian taste and technique. Printed paper fan leaves continued in popularity and the middle years of the century saw many national events which were commemorated by printed paper fans. France took the lead in this sphere, and indeed introduced many innovations and improvements in fan design.

There was a much more international style in fan design and the country of origin can be very difficult to determine. Many materials were used for fans and fashionable size at any one time could vary enormously. Lace returned to popularity and a lace fan was a very fitting accessory for evening dresses, particularly those trimmed with lace. Mother of pearl also became widely used for sticks and guards. Its natural colours could be supplemented by staining, and it could be elaborately carved and pierced. Another popular material for sticks and guards was tortoiseshell. Many technical and industrial advances made possible the production of relatively inexpensive but very decorative fans – the forerunners of plastics, for instance, which imitated tortoiseshell, and machine-made lace.

19 Mahogany brisé fan painted in oil colours by Franz Theyer of Vienna with a design of roses, violets and lilies of the valley round a nest with a baby. It is believed that this fan may mark the first birthday of Princess May of Teck (later Queen Mary) in 1868. It has a matching mahogany box. (right)

20 Brisé fan with fine beech sticks inlaid with white silk, pierced and painted on each side with a design of ivy leaves. The Prince of Wales' crown and crest over intertwined A's on the guards also appear on the lid of the matching box. This fan was a gift to the Princess of Wales, later Queen Alexandra, possibly from her husband (later Edward VII) in the late 1860s. (below)

21 Richly carved and pierced ivory guard from a fan once owned by Alexandra, Princess of Wales; 1865–75. (below, right)

Once a fashionable accessory during the daytime as well as for evening functions, the use of the fan became restricted to evening dress. Hence fine laces, silks and gauzes were particularly appropriate, and exotic feathers began to develop in popularity too. Fans gradually increased in size, becoming exceedingly large in the last two decades of the nineteenth century. The large silk leaves of these fans offered a perfect foil for painted decoration which was often sparing and well executed. More ornately decorated fans of this type also exist, despite many efforts to improve the quality of design and painting on fans through competitions. Not all fans were large and small fans were an equally fashionable alternative.

Smaller fans were indeed returning to favour in the early twentieth century, but the outbreak and aftermath of war so changed society that fans were rapidly discarded as accessories. In polite circles a fan was still 'de rigueur', an especially necessary accessory for presentation at Court where large feather fans, usually white, became usual. One last area of popularity remained, however, for the fan. Printed paper, and occasionally silk, fans had been used for advertising since the late nineteenth century. The 1920s saw the greatest profusion of cheap small paper fans, given away as souvenirs in hotels and restaurants as well as by businesses, intent on advertising their wares as attractively and widely as possible.

22 Large black silk fan of 1875–85 painted with a flock of swallows in grey and white. The sticks and guards are of black stained wood. (above)

23 Tortoiseshell guard from a fan presented to Queen Victoria in 1877 by the Prince of Wales. (right)

24 Evening dresses, from Myra's Journal of Dress and Fashion, December 1884.

25 Fan of fine white gauze painted with irises and butterflies in pale blue, greens, white and black with gold and silver highlights, a personal gift to the Princess of Wales (later Queen Alexandra) on her 25th wedding anniversary on 10 March 1888. Signed by Faucon, Paris; plain mother of pearl sticks and guards.

26 Cream lace fan presented to Princess May of Teck by the lacemakers of Honiton on her marriage to the Duke of York (later George V) in 1893; the mother of pearl sticks have pierced and gilt decoration.

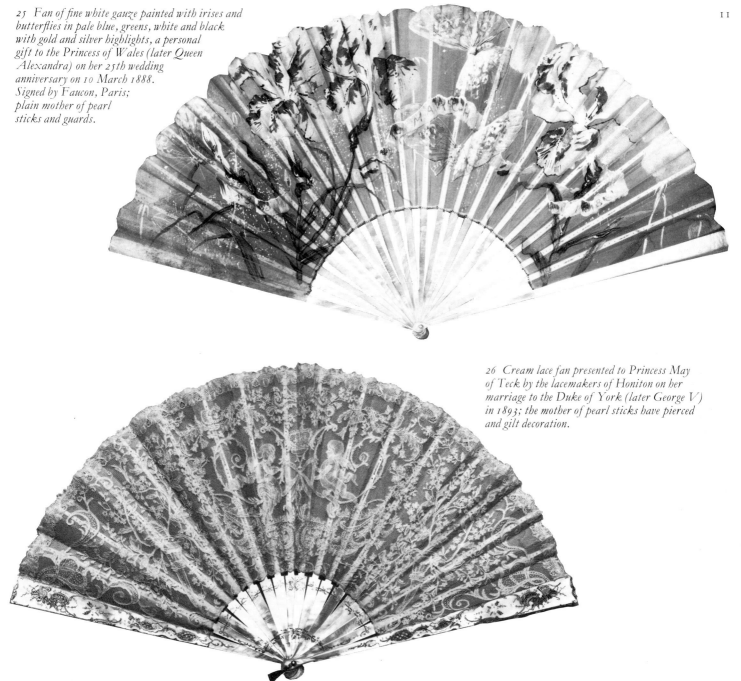

27/28 *Two Court Presentation fans made in the fixed style for convenience. The larger fan of the 1890s is of white ostrich and egret feathers set in a mother of pearl handle. The fan of 1922 has only two feathers set in a finely carved ivory handle. (left)*

Inside cover (right)

Group of twentieth century printed paper advertising fans, free souvenirs from hotels and restaurants. At the top, four 1920s fans from Claridges, the Berkeley, the Carlton, and the New Criterion Restaurant. One of the early twentieth century fans below is from the Savoy, and the others commemorate a performance of 'The Mikado' and leaders of the Boer War (1899–1902) in South Africa.

29 *'Louis Felberman's Celebrity Fan', a printed silk leaf of the 1890s featuring photographs of seventy actors and actresses, with incised bone sticks and guards. (below)*

SELECTED READING

ALEXANDER, H *Fans*, London (1984)
ARMSTRONG, N *A Collector's History of Fans*, London & New York (1974)
ARMSTRONG, N *Fans, A Collector's Guide*, London (1984)
MAYOR, S *Collecting Fans*, London (1980)

ACKNOWLEDGEMENTS

This booklet was published to accompany 'Ivory, Feathers and Lace', an exhibition of the Museum's fan collection, December 1985 to April 1986. The Museum of London acknowledges with appreciation the advice of Santina Levey, Avril Hart and Verity Wilson of the Victoria and Albert Museum in connexion with both. The exhibition was sponsored by the Friends of Fashion of the Museum of London, the Nippon Herald, Guardian Royal Exchange Assurance, the Worshipful Company of Fanmakers of London, and Phillips the Fine Art Auctioneers.